Energy Essentials
Fossil Fuel

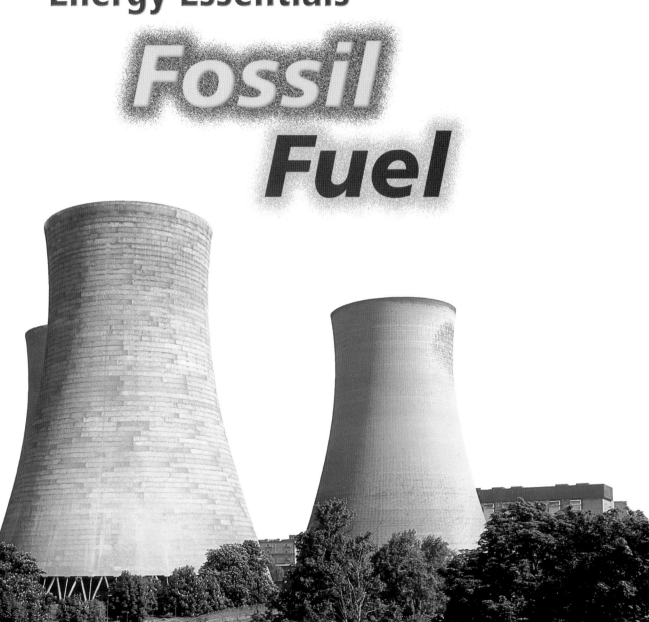

Nigel Saunders and Steven Chapman

Raintree

Chicago, Illinois

© 2004 Raintree
Published by Raintree,
A division of Reed Elsevier, Inc.
Chicago, IL

For information, address the publisher:
Raintree, 100 N. LaSalle, Suite 1200, Chicago, IL 60602

Printed and bound in China
08 07 06 05 04
10 9 8 7 6 5 4 3 2 1

Library of Congress Cataloging-in-Publication Data

Cataloging-in-publication data is available at the Library of Congress.

Acknowledgments

p.**4/5**, Science Photo Library; p.**4**, Science Photo Library/ D. Ouelette, Publiphoto Diffusion; p.**5** (top)Corbis; p.**5** (mid) Science Photo Library; p.**5** (bottom), Science Photo library Zedcor/James Holmes; p.**6/7**, Science Photo Library; p.**6**, Corbis; p.**7**, Science Photo Library/Chris Butler; pp.**8/9**, Alamy; p.**8**, Science Photo Library; p.**9**, Oxford Scientfic Films; pp.**10/11**, Science Photo Library; p.**10**, Corbis; p.**11**, Oxford Scientfic Films; p.**12/13**, Corbis; p.**12**, Corbis; p.**13**, Corbis; p.**14** (top), Heritage Images/ Science Museum/HIP/ Topfoto; p.**14** (bottom), Science Photo Library; p.**15**, Corbis; p.**16** left, Photodisc; p.**16** right, Science Photo Library; p.**17**, Corbis/ Paul A Sonders; p.**18** (top), Science Photo Library; p.**18** (bottom), Oxford Scientfic Films; p.**19**, Corbis; p.**20** (top), Corbis; p.**20** (bottom), Science Photo Library; p.**21**, Rex Features; pp.**22/23**, photodisc; p.**22**, Science Photo Library/Vanessa Vick; p.**24**, Science Photo Library/ Martin Bond; p.**25**, Science Photo library Zedcor/James Holmes; p.**26**, Science Photo Library; p.**27**, Science Photo Library/Ben Johnson; pp.**28/29**, Science Photo Library; p.**29**, Science Photo Library; p.**30** (right), Science Photo Library; p.**30** (left), Science Photo Library; p.**31**, Corbis; p.**32**, Science Photo Library; p.**34** (top), Corbis/ Document General Motors/Reuter R; p.**34** (bottom), Science Photo Library; p.**35**, Science Photo Library/ Simon Fraser; pp.**36/37**, Getty Images News and Sport; pp.**38/39**, Science Photo Library; p.**38**, Getty Images News and Sport; p.**39**, Oxford Scientfic Films; pp.**40–41**, Ecoscene; p.**40**, Science Photo Library; p.**41**, Science Photo Library/ Martin Bond; p.**42** (right), Science Photo Library; p.**42** (left), Getty Images News and Sport; p.**43**, Rex Features/ Stewart Cook.

Cover photograph of gas hob reproduced with permission of Getty Imagebank

Every effort has been made to contact copyright holders of any material reproduced in this book. Any omissions will be rectified in subsequent printings if notice is given to the publishers.

Disclaimer:
All the Internet addresses (URLs) given in this book were valid at the time of going to press. However, due to the dynamic nature of the Internet, some addresses may have changed, or sites may have changed or ceased to exist since publication. While the author and Publishers regret any inconvenience this may cause readers, no responsibility for any such changes can be accepted by either the author or the Publishers.

Contents

Any words appearing in the text in bold, **like this,** are explained in the glossary. You can also look out for them in the "word store" at the bottom of each page.

What Are Fuels?

Good fuels

Lots of substances can be burned, but most of them do not make good fuels. For example, rubber and many plastics burn easily. But they do not make good fuels because they make **poisonous** gases and thick black smoke when they burn.

We are surrounded by **energy.** Heat energy is needed to cook food and keep us warm. Light energy lets us see the words on this page and sound energy allows us to listen to a CD. Energy lets machines and animals move. Energy cannot be destroyed or made out of thin air. But it can change from one form to another.

Fuels are **energy resources.** They give out energy when they burn. Fuels do not make energy—they just store it in a useful form. There are many different fuels, including wood, charcoal, **coal,** gasoline, diesel, and **natural gas.** In this book you will find out about the **fossil fuels.**

FAST FACTS

The unit of energy is the joule, J. It was named after the English scientist James Joule.

When old rubber car tires burn they make thick, black, poisonous smoke. ⋎

Tankers carry huge amounts of crude oil or liquid natural gas around the world. The biggest can carry about a quarter of a million tons. ➤

Word store  energy   ability to do work; light, heat, and electricity are types of energy
extract   remove or take out

What are fossil fuels?

Fossil fuels are coal, **crude oil,** and natural gas. They are called fossil fuels because they formed from the remains of living things that died millions of years ago.

Coal is a black solid made from the remains of ancient plants. It is used as a fuel in power stations. These make the electricity needed to light and heat homes, schools, offices, and factories and to run all sorts of machines.

Crude oil is a thick, smelly liquid formed from the remains of ancient sea creatures. Fuels such as gasoline and diesel are **extracted** from crude oil. Natural gas also formed millions of years ago from the remains of sea creatures. It is a colorless gas that is often burned in homes for cooking and heating.

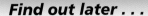

Find out later . . .

How do machines dig for coal?

What do gigantic oil platforms do?

What else are fossil fuels used for?

fuel   substance that stores energy and releases it when it is burned
poisonous   substance that makes us ill or even kills us

Coal

This is a very wet modern swamp. ʌ

What is a swamp?

Wetlands are areas with very wet soil. Sometimes they are totally covered by water because the ground is flat and does not drain well. Both swamps and marshes are types of wetland. Swamps contain many trees, but marshes have few trees.

Coal formed from the remains of trees and other plants that died around 300 million years ago. The world was a very different place then.

From sunlight to huge forests

There were no people 300 million years ago. Even dinosaurs did not yet exist. It was much warmer then, and the world was covered by huge, swampy forests. But how did some of these forests become coal?

Plants make their own food using a process called **photosynthesis.** A green substance in their leaves called **chlorophyll** traps light **energy** from the Sun. This energy is used to change water from the soil and carbon dioxide from the air into **glucose** and other sugars. Because it was warmer 300 million years ago and there was more carbon in the atmosphere, plants grew very quickly.

Word store   carboniferous   coal-producing
chemical reaction   change in which new substances are made

From huge forests to coal

Photosynthesis let the **carboniferous** plants turn light energy into chemical energy, which was stored in the plants in sugars. Over time, this chemical energy became stored in coal.

When the trees and other plants in the forests died, the swampy conditions stopped them from rotting away. Thick layers of dead plants formed, one on top of the other. These were slowly buried by layers of mud and sand. Over thousands of years, the weight of the mud and sand crushed the buried plants.

Chemical reactions and the heat of Earth slowly warmed the crushed plants and turned them into coal. Fifty feet (15 meters) of dead trees and plants would become a 3.3 foot- (1-meter) layer of coal. Different types of coal formed, depending on how deeply the plant material was buried and how long the chemical reactions continued.

The dinosaurs existed millions of years after the coal-forming forests. ∧

Earth in one day

Earth formed about 4.6 **billion** years ago. Imagine that this time was crushed into just one day. On that scale, the first living things appeared 19 hours ago. The coal-forming swamps existed 90 minutes ago, and humans appeared just one second ago.

The time when the coal-forming swamps existed, from 360 to 280 million years ago, is called the **Carboniferous period.** ≺

photosynthesis   process by which plants use light energy to convert carbon dioxide and water into sugars and oxygen

Slabs of peat are cut from a trench and stacked in heaps to dry. One-third of Ireland's electricity is made by burning peat. ʌ

Peat

Peat is the remains of **bog** plants that have been rotting and crushed for thousands of years. It is soft and brown and contains bits of roots and leaves. It can be cut with a shovel, dried, and then used as a **fuel.** Peat makes a lot of ash and smoke when it burns.

Types of coal

All **coal** was formed from the remains of ancient plants, but there are different types, called **ranks.** The ranks of coal look different and do not burn in the same way. They also give off different amounts of useful **energy** when they burn.

Top ranking

Carbon is the main **element** in coal. Other elements, such as hydrogen and oxygen, are also present. The best coals contain the most carbon. In these coals, more of the changes have occurred that turn dead plants into coal. High-ranking **coals give off the most heat energy when they burn. They also make the least amount of smoke and soot.**

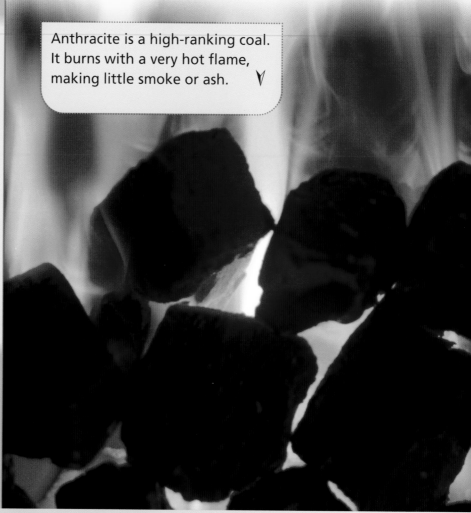

Anthracite is a high-ranking coal. It burns with a very hot flame, making little smoke or ash. ⱽ

Word store   bog   waterlogged and spongy wetland
element   substance made of only one kind of atom

Lignite

Lignite is the lowest-ranking coal. It is often called brown coal. It contains the most moisture and the least carbon of all coals. It also gives off the least energy and the most smoke when it burns. Lignite is used mainly in power stations to make electricity.

Bituminous coal

Bituminous coal is the most common rank of coal. It can be soft and powdery, hard and shiny, or a mixture of the two types. Bituminous coal contains more carbon than lignite. It burns with a hot but smoky flame.

Anthracite

Anthracite is nearly pure carbon. It is the highest-ranking coal and also the least common. It is black, hard, and shiny. Although anthracite is difficult to light, it burns with a very hot and smokeless flame and releases the most energy.

Leaves in the lumps

In some lumps of coal you can see wood patterns from the trees that made them. **Fossilized** pieces of leaf are also found in coal. These are very interesting to scientists who want to learn about ancient plants.

FAST FACTS

In 2001, 5.2 billion tons of coal were **mined** around the world—enough to give every person on the planet about four-fifths of a ton.

A fossilized leaf in a piece of coal.

fossilized   turned into stone
rank   type of coal

Peat is found at Earth's surface, but **coal** is usually found deep underground. As the coal formed, the layers of mud and sand that covered it turned into rock. So coal must be **mined** to get it out of the ground. The type of mining used depends on how deeply the coal is buried.

Scrape it off

Surface mining is used where the coal **seams** are less than 265 feet (80 meters) under the surface. The first stage in surface mining is to take away the soil and rock that lie on **top of the coal. The soil and rock are stored and put back after the coal has been dug out.**

Bucket wheels and draglines

Huge machines are needed for surface mining. The biggest are the bucket wheels and draglines used to remove soil and rock. They weigh thousands of tons and some can move 350,00 cu ft (10,000 cu m) of soil an hour. This is enough soil to fill three Olympic swimming pools.

A surface mine in Germany. Huge machines dig out the coal to use in nearby power stations. ➤

This huge machine scoops up 3,200 cu ft (90 cu m) of soil and rock in one try. ⋁

coal   black, solid fossil fuel
mine   dig out of the ground

Dig it out

After the soil and rock have been scraped away, the coal is dug up. The mine might have deep pits or shallow strips, depending on where the coal seam is and if there are things like villages in the way. Power stations are often built near coal mines. This means that the coal is close to the place where it is used as a **fuel**.

Land reclaimed after surface coal mining. ∧

Surface mining

Benefits
- Surface mining is much safer for miners than underground mining.

Problems
- Surface mining damages large areas of land and spoils the view.
- People who live nearby may have to move to new homes to make way for the mines.
- It destroys the habitat of local plants and animals.

Reclaiming the land

To reduce the damage done to the environment by surface mining, the land is **reclaimed**. The stored rock and soil are put back. New trees, bushes, and grasses are planted to replace those destroyed by the mine.

FAST FACTS

Surface mining is also called opencast mining or strip mining.

reclaim make something useful again
seam layer of coal

Children used to be allowed to work in coal mines. ∧

Digging deep

Surface **mining** is only worth doing if the **coal seam** is near the surface. If a seam is too deep, underground mining has to be done instead. About two-thirds of the world's coal is mined using underground mining.

Deep mining

Underground mining is also called deep mining. To reach the coal seam, deep holes called **shafts** are dug down into Earth's **crust.** Miners take the equipment they need down these shafts. They dig coal from the seam and bring it up to the surface through **the shafts. Modern mines use machines to cut the coal and conveyor belts to move it from the coalface to the shafts.**

A dark history

For many years miners had only pickaxes for digging coal. Women and children worked with the men in the coal mines. In 1842 the British government banned children under ten years old and women from working underground.

coalface   part of a coal seam that is being cut away
shaft   narrow vertical hole

Room and pillar mining

If a whole coal seam were just dug out, the ceiling of the mine would fall in and the land above it would sink. To stop this from happening, thick pillars of coal are left behind. These support a network of "rooms" in which the coal has been taken away. But it means that only about half the coal in a seam can be mined.

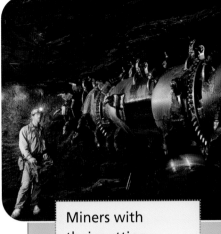

Miners with their cutting equipment in a longwall mine.

Underground mining

Benefits

- Underground mining does less damage to the land than surface mining.

Problems

- It is more dangerous for miners.
- Waste rock from underground is piled up on the surface as **spoil heaps**. These need to be planted with trees and bushes to improve the environment.

This cutting tool in a deep mine cuts away sections of coal 28 in. (70 cm) deep and 720 ft (220 m) long.

Longwall mining

Some countries also use longwall mining. Spinning blades cut a wide coalface while the roof is held up with machines. After the coal has been taken away, the roof is allowed to cave in. More coal can be taken away using this method, but the land above the mine often **subsides**.

FAST FACTS

Mining can be a very dangerous job. In 1906, 1,100 miners were killed when a French coal mine caught fire.

spoil heap   pile of waste material from a mine
subside   sink downward

Getting steamed up

There are all sorts of machines in the modern world. It is very difficult to imagine life without them. But just over 200 years ago, there were very few engines and no trains or tractors. At the start of the 19th century, **coal** began to change this.

The Industrial Revolution was the time when several countries began to change from making things on a small scale to making them in large factories. The invention of steam-powered machinery was very important for the Industrial Revolution. It meant that workers could make more goods, and these goods could be **transported** faster. **Coal was the fuel used in steam engines, trains, and ships.**

This is a model of James Watt's steam engine. ∧

Steam engines

In 1712 Thomas Newcomen used the steam engine he had designed to pump water out of **mines**. James Watt, a Scottish engineer, **patented** an even better design in 1769. This steam engine could also run factory machinery. The unit of power was named after James Watt.

Coal was the **fuel** for many steam-powered machines, such as steam trains. ➤

acid rain   rain that contains more acid than normal; it damages buildings and living things

Engines everywhere

During the 1800s and early 1900s, factories made all sorts of goods using steam power. Steam trains moved goods and people across the countryside, while steam ships took them all over the world. There were even steam-powered tractors and trucks. Coal fueled the Industrial Revolution, but it also brought problems.

Black smoke everywhere

When coal burns, some of the carbon in it escapes as smoke. Smoke in the air makes it difficult to breathe, and it turns buildings black. Some sulfur is also found in coal, and it forms sulfur dioxide when the coal burns. This gas **dissolves** in clouds to form harmful **acid rain**. By the middle of the 20th century, substances from burning coal had begun to harm the environment.

Killer fog

In December 1952 air **pollution** from coal burning in London became deadly. Smoke from homes and factories mixed with fog to make a thick, black **smog**. This lasted for four days and killed around 4,000 people.

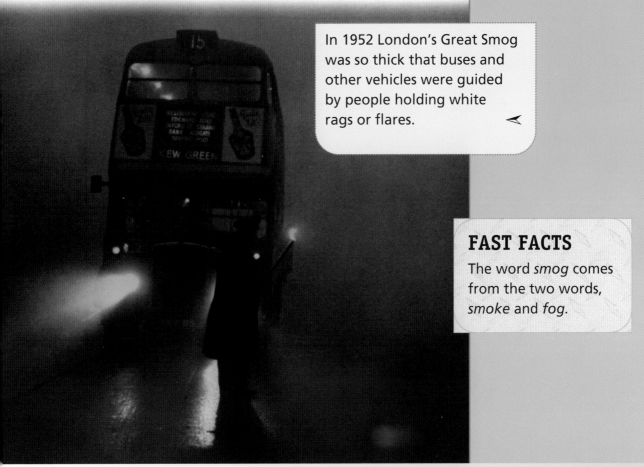

In 1952 London's Great Smog was so thick that buses and other vehicles were guided by people holding white rags or flares.

FAST FACTS

The word *smog* comes from the two words, *smoke* and *fog*.

Coal-fired power stations are usually built close to coalfields because they need regular supplies of coal to keep them running. ˅

Stop it from escaping

Smoke from coal contains ash and sulfur dioxide gas. These cause breathing problems and **acid rain.** Coal-fired power stations now have filters fitted to their smokestacks. These stop most of the ash and sulfur dioxide from escaping, but they make the power stations less efficient.

Smoke pollution pours out of smokestacks. ʌ

Using coal today

The use of **coal** is increasing. Some is still used to **fuel** steam-powered machines or heat homes, but there are many other uses.

Coal as a fuel

Limestone is a rock that is used to make cement. It needs to be heated strongly, and coal is the most common fuel used in cement factories. But the biggest use of coal today is in power stations that make electricity.

In a power station, coal is burned in boilers to give off heat **energy.** This boils water to make steam. The steam turns a **turbine** and this turns a **generator** to make the electricity. Coal-fired power stations make over a third of the world's electricity. But they are not very **efficient.** Only about 35 percent of the chemical energy stored in the coal is turned into electricity. Most of the rest is wasted as heat energy that escapes into the environment.

But coal is not just used as a fuel.

efficient   good at doing useful things with the energy it gets
generator   equipment used to make electricity

Chemical coal

If coal is heated strongly, it breaks down into coal gas, coal tar, and coke. Coal gas, sometimes called town gas, is a smelly mixture of gases. It can be used instead of natural gas for heating and lighting. Coal tar is a mixture of over a hundred different substances. A lot of these are very useful. They are used to make dyes, paints, varnish, explosives, soaps, medicines, and **pesticides.** One of the substances in coal tar is the thick black tar used to make roads and to waterproof roofs.

FAST FACTS
Five percent of all the coal used in the world is burned in homes for cooking and heating.

Not for drinking . . .
Coke is a black solid made by heating coal. It is pure carbon and makes a very good fuel. When coke burns, it gives off more heat and much less smoke than coal. It is used to make blast furnaces hot enough to **extract** iron from iron ore.

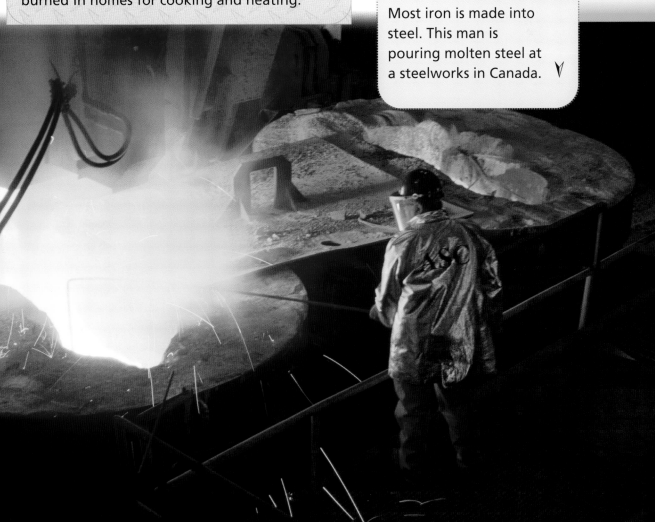

Most iron is made into steel. This man is pouring molten steel at a steelworks in Canada.

pesticide   chemical that kills insects and other pests that harm crops
turbine   machinery that is turned by moving air, water, or steam

Oil

The oil used to **lubricate** bicycle chains is just one of the many substances that come from **crude oil.** Crude oil itself can be anything from a pale yellow color to black. It is a mixture of different liquids, with solids and gases **dissolved** in it. Just like **coal,** crude oil formed from the remains of living things that died millions of years ago. But these were not plants in a swampy forest.

Prehistoric seas

When tiny sea creatures died millions of years ago, they sank to the seabed. Over time, they were covered by layers of mud and sand and crushed. **Chemical reactions** slowly warmed up the remains and turned them into oil.

Droplets of oil float on water and do not mix with it. ⋀

Crude oil is a thick, smelly mixture of liquids, solids, and gases. ⋎

Oil and water do not mix

Puddles on roads often have swirling patterns of color on their surface. These are caused by oil, gasoline, or diesel that has leaked from cars. Oil does not dissolve in water and it has a lower **density** than water, so a thin layer of oil floats on puddles.

Word store   crude oil   liquid fossil fuel with various solids and gases dissolved in it
density   measure of how heavy something is compared to its size

Oil fields

As the remains of the dead sea creatures slowly turned into oil, the layers of mud and sand on top of them turned into rock. Some of the rocks were full of tiny holes and cracks, a bit like a sponge. Water deep underground pushed the oil upward through these **porous** rocks. Sometimes the oil got all the way up to the surface. When this happened, tar sands and tar pits were formed.

Most of the time, the layers of porous rocks were covered by layers of **nonporous** rocks. These rocks did not have any holes and cracks, so they stopped the oil from reaching the surface. Large amounts of oil were trapped underground, forming oil fields.

The bones of sabertoothed tigers and other ancient animals can be found in tar pits.

lubricate   to reduce friction
porous   lets liquids and gases through

Finding oil

Deep holes must be drilled into the ground to get at the oil trapped in an oil field. But oil fields are not found everywhere. Even when an oil field is discovered, if there is not enough oil to make a profit, it is not brought up to the surface.

Detective work

Geologists are scientists who study the different types of rock in Earth's **crust**. To find oil fields, geologists look at lots of information about the rocks in different places. They look for areas where oil could be trapped under **nonporous** rock. The best sites are where the rock is curved upward to make a dome, which means that a lot of oil could be trapped under it.

Satellites in space can collect information about the rocks in **remote** places on Earth.

High-tech hunting

Back on the ground, geologists set off small explosions and use sensitive machines to listen for echoes from deep beneath the surface. Computers use these echoes to figure out the shape of the underground rocks. This is called "seismic surveying."

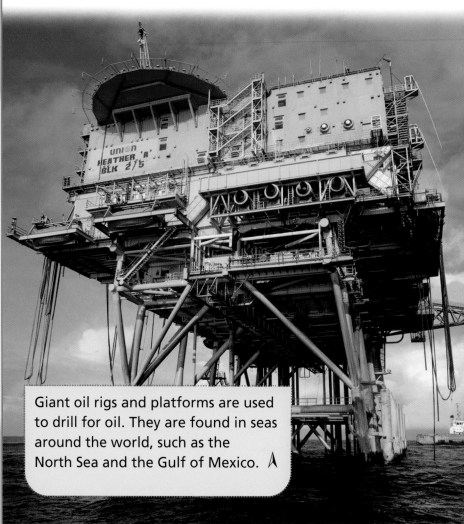

Giant oil rigs and platforms are used to drill for oil. They are found in seas around the world, such as the North Sea and the Gulf of Mexico.

Word store   blowout   dangerous and uncontrolled escape of oil from a well
geologist   scientist who studies rocks

Getting the oil

Once geologists have found a likely place to drill for oil, test holes are drilled from a drilling rig. There may only be a 1-in-50 chance of actually finding oil. Special drills are used to cut through the rock and get to the oil. The drills are tipped with tiny diamonds. Diamond is a very hard form of carbon that can cut through rock. Some wells are hundreds of feet deep.

The oil well is then lined with steel to stop it from collapsing. The top of the well is sealed with powerful **valves** to stop **blowouts.** Some oil fields are underwater. Huge concrete and steel platforms are used to drill down and collect oil ready to send to refineries. This is where the **crude oil** is separated into the different products we use.

Gusher!

Sometimes oil is at such a high pressure that it is forced out of the well and sprays over the drilling rig like a fountain. In the past, blowouts such as this were common and were called gushers. In 1979 over four million **barrels** of oil spilled into the Gulf of Mexico after a blowout from an oil well. With modern drilling methods, gushers are rare.

This 1979 blowout happened underwater. Oil burned on the surface of the ocean. ⋀

remote   far away from towns and cities
valve   device for controlling the movement of liquid or gas through a pipe

21

Crude oil is moved from oil wells to oil refineries using long pipelines or ships called oil tankers. Sometimes oil tankers have accidents and spill their oil. When this happens, thick, sticky oil **pollutes** the ocean, kills wildlife, and ruins beaches.

These people are trying to clean a beach after an oil tanker accident.

Oil refining

Crude oil straight from a well is not ready to be used because it is a mixture of many different substances. It has to be treated at an oil refinery to **extract** useful **fuels** and other substances from it.

Distillation

Steam from a boiling kettle turns back into droplets of water if it hits a cold surface such as a window. This is an example of distillation. A similar process happens at a refinery to the different substances in oil.

At the oil refinery

Crude oil is heated to about 662 °F (350 °C). It is pumped into the bottom of a tall metal fractionating tower. This is **very hot at the bottom but cold at the top.** Substances in the oil **evaporate** and their **vapors** rise up the tower. When they get cold enough, the vapors turn back into liquids and can be collected.

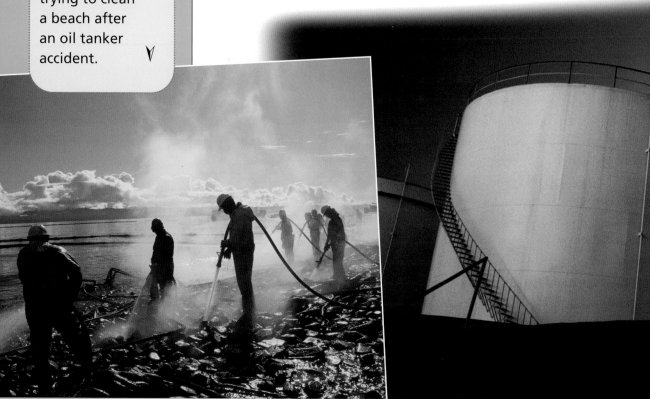

Word store   condense   to change from gas to liquid
fraction   group of substances in crude oil

Fractions

Different substances in crude oil have different boiling points. As the crude oil is heated, substances with high boiling points stay near the bottom of the tower. But the vapors of substances with low boiling points rise to the top. Each group **condenses** and is collected at a different height. These groups are called **fractions.** Each fraction of crude oil contains several useful substances.

Solids, such as the tar used to make roads, have high boiling points and stay at the bottom. Gases, such as the propane used in camping gas, have low boiling points and rise to the top. Liquids, such as gasoline and diesel, turn to vapor and rise to the middle of the tower, where they cool, condense, and are collected.

The different fractions have only been separated from each other. **They have not been changed by any chemical reactions.**

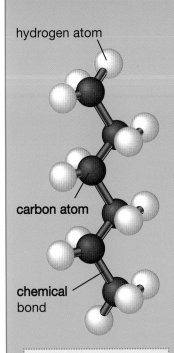

hydrogen atom

carbon atom

chemical bond

This is a model of a hexane molecule, a hydrocarbon found in crude oil.

FAST FACTS
The type of distillation used at oil refineries is called fractional distillation.

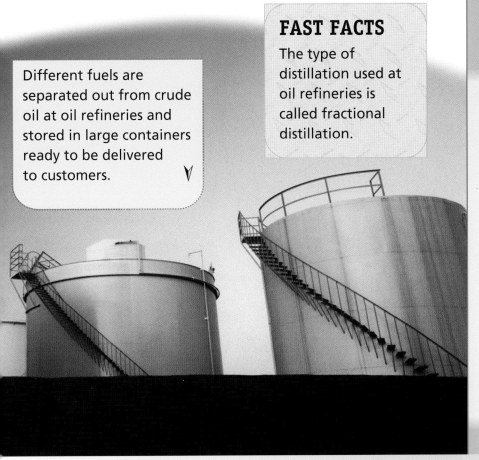

Different fuels are separated out from crude oil at oil refineries and stored in large containers ready to be delivered to customers.

Hydrocarbons
The different substances in oil are mostly **hydrocarbons**. This means that their **molecules** are made from hydrogen and carbon **atoms** only. Small hydrocarbon molecules form gases, medium-sized hydrocarbon molecules form liquids, and long hydrocarbon molecules form solids.

This equipment "cracks" crude oil fractions. ∧

Oil for almost everything

The different **fractions** separated from **crude oil** at oil refineries have an amazing range of uses. Many are good **fuels,** but others are very important **raw materials** for the chemical industry.

The residue

The fraction from the bottom of the fractionating tower is called the residue. It contains a black solid called bitumen. This is used to make road surfaces and to waterproof roofs. The residue also contains the paraffin waxes. These solids are used to make candles, polishes, and greaseproof paper. A very thick liquid called fuel oil can be separated from the residue. Fuel oil is not runny enough to use in cars and trucks, but it is a good fuel for ships and power stations.

Fuels for land and air

Most cars are fueled by gasoline. Diesel oil is used as a fuel for trains, trucks, buses, and some cars. It burns less easily than gasoline and cannot be used in ordinary gasoline engines. Kerosene is used as jet fuel for aircraft. Gasoline and kerosene are very runny and burn easily compared to fuel oil.

Refinery gas

The fraction that comes off the top of the fractionating tower contains four gases. Two of them, propane and butane, are easily turned into liquids by putting them under pressure in metal containers. They are used as bottled fuel for camping stoves. Butane is also used in some refrigerators and aerosol spray cans. Ethane is used as a raw material by the chemical industry. Methane is the main gas found in **natural gas.**

Get cracking!

Crude oil often contains many substances with high boiling points. These make poor fuels. Heating these substances strongly under pressure changes them into more useful substances with lower boiling points, such as gasoline. This is called cracking.

natural gas   colorless fossil fuel gas, mostly methane
raw material   substance that is turned into a final product

These are the main fractions separated from crude oil at an oil refinery. ⋁

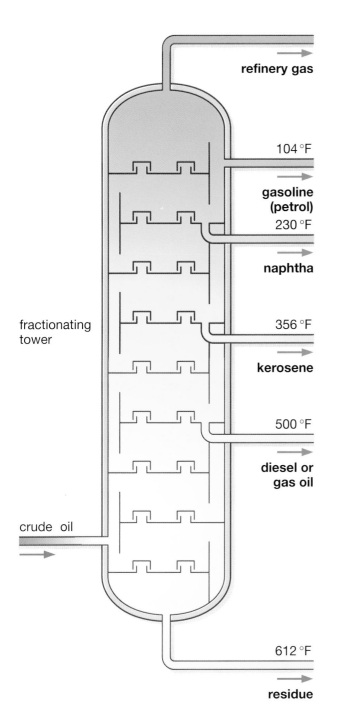

refinery gas

104 °F

gasoline (petrol)

230 °F

naphtha

fractionating tower

356 °F

kerosene

500 °F

diesel or gas oil

crude oil

612 °F

residue

Polythene sheeting being made for the building industry. ⋀

Making things with oil

The naphtha fraction is the raw material for making many useful substances. These include detergents, man-made rubber, medicines, and explosives. Man-made fibers for clothing and plastics such as polythene are made using naphtha.

Natural Gas

A scientist tests for natural gas at a vent in a landfill garbage dump. ∧

Natural **gas** is mostly methane. It is usually formed at the same time as **crude oil,** but there are other ways in which it can be made.

Crude oil and natural gas

The same processes that form crude oil also form natural gas. But higher temperatures and pressures were needed to turn the remains of ancient living things into natural gas. The deeper down the remains are buried, the higher the temperature becomes and the more they are crushed by the rocks above. This means that crude oil and natural gas are found together close to the surface, but deep underground the remains may all have turned to natural gas.

The methods used to get crude oil from the ground are also used to **extract** natural gas. Gas fields can be under the land or seabed.

Biogas

Our intestines contain **bacteria** that can make methane. Bacteria also give off methane when they break down animal waste and the remains of dead plants and animals. Enough natural gas is sometimes released by rotting waste in **landfill** garbage dumps to make it worth collecting for sale.

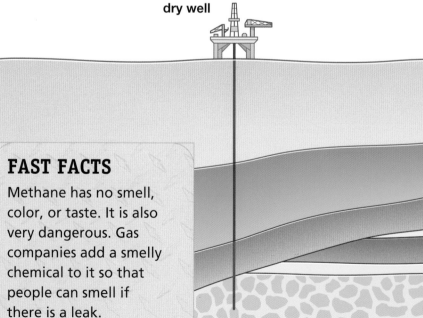

dry well

FAST FACTS

Methane has no smell, color, or taste. It is also very dangerous. Gas companies add a smelly chemical to it so that people can smell if there is a leak.

bacteria   tiny living things
fossil fuel   fuel formed from the remains of ancient plants and animals

Transporting natural gas

Gas fields can be under high pressure, so powerful **valves** are fitted to the tops of wells to keep the natural gas under control. It is sent through pipelines from the gas fields to a refinery.

At the refinery, the natural gas is separated from any crude oil or water that might have come from the ground with it. It is then cooled so that any propane or butane it contains will become liquid. These liquids are separated and stored under pressure in metal containers, ready for sale.

The remaining gas is mainly methane with small amounts of ethane. It is treated to remove any hydrogen sulfide gas, which is **poisonous,** very smelly, and damages pipelines. Most gas is sent from the refinery in pipelines, but sometimes it is cooled to around -255 °F (–160 °C) to make liquid natural gas. This is **transported** in refrigerated tankers.

Safety flames underground

Natural gas is also given off in **coal mines.** It can slowly fill a mine or escape very suddenly. If it comes into contact with a flame, it explodes. This was a big problem for the first miners, who had to take burning lamps underground for light. The English scientist Sir Humphry Davy invented a safety lamp for miners in 1815.

Natural gas and crude oil are often found together. A layer of **nonporous** rock always lies above them, trapping the **fossil fuels** underground.

productive well

nonporous rock

gas

oil

porous rock

water pushes the gas and oil upwards

The flame in a Davy safety lamp was surrounded by layers of **wire gauze** that stopped the flame's heat from escaping.

landfill   waste site
wire gauze   fine metal mesh

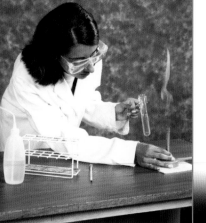

When you use a laboratory Bunsen burner, always wear eye protection and never leave the burner unattended while it is lit.

Using gas

When **natural gas** leaves a refinery, it begins a journey through a branching network of pipelines to reach homes, offices, and factories. Gas pipelines are usually buried underground. The widest pipes carry gas across large distances. They are made of steel and may be over 3 ft (1 m) wide. These branch off at towns and cities, becoming narrower at each branch until they end at a house, office, or factory. The smaller pipes are often made from yellow polyethylene. This is a plastic made from **crude oil** that does not react with the gas.

Push it through

Big machines called **compressors** get the gas moving in the pipelines at about 23 ft (7 m) per second. The gas starts at a **very high pressure, but this falls by the end of the journey.**

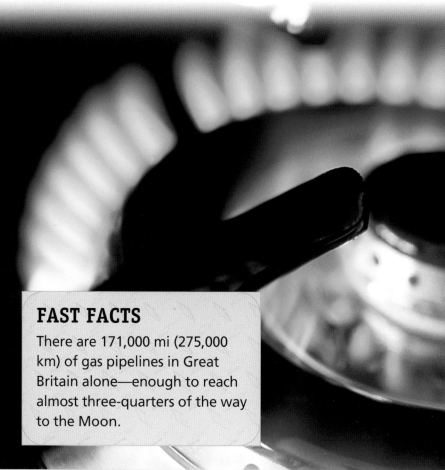

Bunsen burner

In the middle of the 19th century, the German scientists Gustav Kirchhoff and Robert Bunsen needed a very hot flame for their experiments. A **technician** at their university designed a new burner that used natural gas. It became known as the Bunsen burner.

FAST FACTS

There are 171,000 mi (275,000 km) of gas pipelines in Great Britain alone—enough to reach almost three-quarters of the way to the Moon.

compressor   type of pump

Uses of natural gas

In homes, schools, offices, restaurants, and hotels:

- cooking;
- heating water;
- running air-conditioning systems.

In factories:

- heating;
- air-conditioning;
- to produce the heat needed to make bricks, tiles, and glass;
- as a **raw material** for making chemicals such as ammonia, used in **fertilizers.**

In gas-fired power stations:

- as a **fuel** to make electricity. Combined heat and power stations not only make electricity—they use any waste **heat to keep nearby houses warm.**

Driving with gas

Natural gas can be used to fuel vehicles. To store enough of it, the gas is kept under pressure or as a liquid in the fuel tank. There are not many refueling stations, so natural gas is most popular with buses, which can refill at special gas stations.

This bus is fueled by natural gas. ∧

Natural gas is a fuel for household stoves. ∧

fertilizer   chemical that gives plants the minerals they need to grow well
technician   someone who helps scientists do their work

Problems with Fossil Fuels

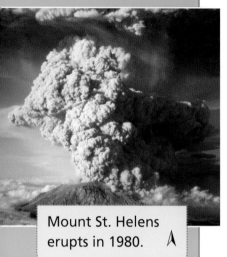

Mount St. Helens erupts in 1980. ∧

You may have heard the terms **acid rain, global warming,** and **pollution.** All these things are caused when we burn **fossil fuels.** And there is another problem: fossil fuels are quickly running out. We have to find new sources of **energy** for the future and also make sure that using the remaining fossil fuels does not damage the planet forever.

Beware of the rain

When fossil fuels burn, the carbon and hydrogen form carbon dioxide and water **vapor.** Fossil fuels also contain small amounts of sulfur, which reacts with oxygen in the air to make sulfur dioxide. This gas has a sharp smell. It brings on asthma attacks and damages the lungs. Sulfur dioxide also **dissolves** in the clouds to make rain more **acidic.**

Volcano!

Sulfur dioxide is given off naturally by volcanoes. Mount St. Helens in Washington state gave off 441,000 tons (400,000 tonnes) of sulfur dioxide when it erupted in 1980, and Mount Pinatubo in the Philippines gave off 19 million tons (17 million tonnes) in 1991. But large volcanoes do not erupt very often. Power stations give off over 11 million tons (10 million tonnes) of sulfur dioxide each year.

Waste gases from burning fossil fuels make acid rain. This damages buildings, statues, and living things. ➢

Word store   dilute   mixed with another substance, usually water
mineral   substance needed by plants and animals to keep them healthy

Acid rain

Half of the sulfur dioxide given off by human activities comes from burning **coal**. About 25 percent comes from burning fuels made from **crude oil**. Sulfur dioxide dissolves in water droplets in the clouds to form **dilute** sulfuric acid. This falls to the ground in rain. Acid rain can be even more acidic than lemon juice.

Acid rain reacts with metals, making them wear away more quickly. It reacts with stone, damaging the surface of buildings and statues. Acid rain also harms living things. It dissolves **minerals** in the soil. It washes them away before plants can use them to grow properly. In areas where acid rain falls, trees lose their leaves and cannot stand up to **pests** and diseases. When acid rain falls in rivers and lakes, it kills plants and animals.

Beating acid rain

The best way to beat acid rain is to stop sulfur dioxide from escaping. The smoke from burning fossil fuels can be filtered, or the sulfur can be taken away from the fuels before they are burned. The next best thing is to **neutralize** the acid rain after it has fallen, using powdered lime or limestone.

Acid in this Swedish lake is being neutralized using powdered lime.

neutralize   to make a substance neutral so it does not react with metals or rocks
pest   insect or fungus that damages plants

In the greenhouse

The average temperature on Earth's surface is 59 °F (15 °C). The Moon is the same distance from the Sun as Earth, but its average temperature is just 0 °C (−18 °C), about the same as a freezer. Why is Earth warm when the Moon is cold?

The greenhouse effect

Some of the Sun's **energy** escapes into space after it hits Earth's surface. This also happens on the Moon, but Earth has an atmosphere, while the Moon does not. Some of the gases in Earth's atmosphere, such as carbon dioxide, are very good at trapping heat energy. These gases are called greenhouse gases. They stop some of the heat from escaping and keep Earth warm. This warming is called the **greenhouse effect.** Without it, Earth would be too cold for anything to live.

Methane is also given off by rice fields. ⋀

Cows and rice fields

Carbon dioxide is not the only gas that is good at trapping heat in the atmosphere. Methane does it, too. Methane is the main gas found in **natural gas.** It is also given off in large amounts by cows and rice fields.

Gases in the atmosphere trap heat and keep Earth warm, like glass traps heat in a greenhouse. ➤

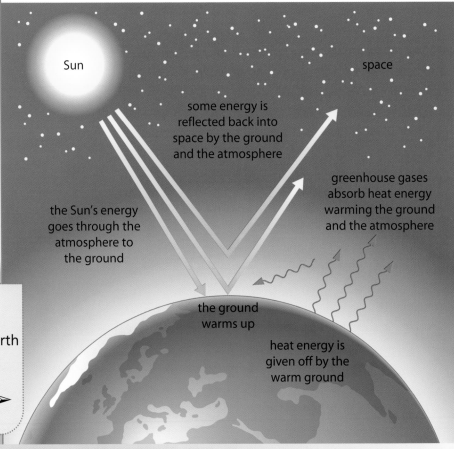

Sun

space

some energy is reflected back into space by the ground and the atmosphere

greenhouse gases absorb heat energy warming the ground and the atmosphere

the Sun's energy goes through the atmosphere to the ground

the ground warms up

heat energy is given off by the warm ground

global warming   extra warming of Earth caused by an increased greenhouse effect

Global warming

Earth is slowly becoming much warmer than it would be if humans were not living on the planet. This is because the use of **fossil fuels** has put much more carbon dioxide into the atmosphere. The extra carbon dioxide traps more heat than usual and makes the greenhouse effect stronger than it would be naturally. This is **global warming,** and it is already starting to cause problems.

Melting in the heat

As Earth warms up, the **polar ice caps** will melt. Sea levels will rise, flooding lowland areas. The weather will change. Some parts of the world will get more rain while other parts will get less rain. Crops will not grow where they do now.

Going up

The concentration of carbon dioxide in the atmosphere went up from 0.028 percent in 1850 to about 0.037 percent at the start of this century. This may not seem like much, but during that time, average temperatures at Earth's surface went up by around 2 °F (1 °C). The carbon dioxide concentration and temperature are still going up.

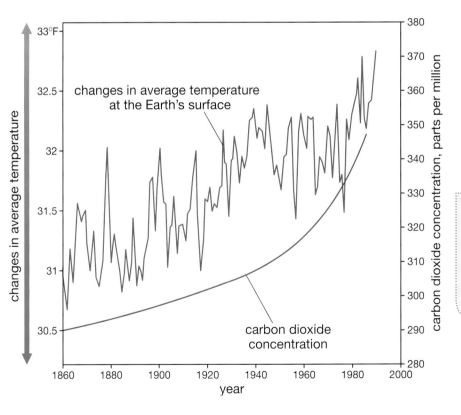

As the concentration of carbon dioxide in the atmosphere has gone up, so has the average temperature.

greenhouse effect   how Earth's atmosphere keeps the planet warm
polar ice caps   ice covering the north and south poles of Earth

These are catalytic converters, cut open so you can see inside them. ∧

Catalytic converters

Catalytic converters are fitted to car exhaust systems to change some of the polluting gases into less harmful ones. They contain a honeycomb coated with a thin layer of platinum, rhodium, and palladium. These metals speed up the **chemical reactions** that convert **polluting** gases into other substances.

Busy streets

When gasoline or diesel burn in an unlimited supply of oxygen, the only wastes they make are carbon dioxide and water **vapor.** It is very different when they burn in an engine.

Exhaust fumes

There is not much air in an engine. This means that there is not enough oxygen for the **fuel** to burn completely. Extra waste substances are made, including carbon monoxide and smelly fumes from small amounts of unburned fuel. An engine can get so hot that nitrogen and oxygen from the air react together. They make gases called nitrogen oxides.

These waste gases come out through the exhaust pipe. Carbon monoxide is a **poisonous** gas. The unburned fuel reacts with gases in the air to make **smog,** and the nitrogen oxides dissolve in clouds to make **acid rain.**

The waste gases from vehicle exhaust pipes are unpleasant and pollute the air we breathe. ∨

catalytic converter   equipment attached to a vehicle exhaust system to reduce the amount of harmful gases given out

More problems

Catalytic converters cut down the amount of harmful gases that are given out by cars and other vehicles. But as they do this, they make more carbon dioxide. This is a greenhouse gas, and it adds to **global warming.** And even with catalytic converters, the use of **fossil fuels** in cities can make smog, especially in the summer.

At ground level, ozone is a gas that causes stinging eyes and breathing problems. Sunlight makes the different substances in exhaust fumes react with air to make ozone. This is a big problem for people in cities during summer days. Ozone **pollution** can also travel to the countryside on the wind, where it damages growing crops.

Modern smog

During the Industrial Revolution, smog was mostly just a mixture of smoke and fog. But modern smog contains more substances. Many of these react in sunlight to make even more harmful substances. Smog can travel hundreds of miles from the cities where it forms.

FAST FACTS

Ozone high in the atmosphere shields us from harmful **ultraviolet light** from the Sun.

This smog has traveled hundreds of miles from the city of Los Angeles, California.

pollution   harmful substances in the air, water, or land
ultraviolet light   invisible light that can damage skin, eyes, and growing plants

35

Type of fossil fuel	Coal	Crude oil	Natural gas
Amount left in the ground	1 trillion tons	1 trillion barrels	5.5 **trillion** cubic feet
Amount used each day	13.1 million tons	74 million barrels	247 **billion** cubic feet
Time left until it runs out	214 years	39 years	61 years

We will run out of crude oil first. ⋀

Some guesses
If we know roughly how much of each fossil fuel is left and how quickly it is being used, we can guess how long it should last. There are about 214 years of coal, 39 years of crude oil, and 61 years of natural gas left.

Dripping dry
Fossil fuels cause **pollution,** but could we manage without them? We will have to survive without them one day because they are running out. The fossil fuels are **nonrenewable energy resources.** This means that once they have been used up, they will be gone forever. So how long do we have before they run out?

A tricky problem
It is difficult to be sure when the fossil fuels will run out. It depends how quickly we can find alternative energy resources. It is also difficult to be sure just how many tons of **coal, barrels** of **crude oil,** and cubic feet of **natural gas** are left.

A taste of things to come? Fossil fuels will run out one day. ➢

Arctic   far north, where it is usually very cold
barrel   unit used to measure the volume of crude oil; one barrel is 42 gal (159 l)

Top of the hill

New coal, oil, and gas fields continue to be discovered. This puts off the time when the fossil fuels will run out. But each year, fewer new supplies are discovered, and the world is using up fossil fuels more quickly. The estimated amount of time left before the fossil fuels finally run out has gone down steadily since 1990.

As fossil fuels begin to run out, their price will go up. Supplies that are difficult and expensive to reach at the moment will become worth getting. Many of these are in **remote** places, such as **the Arctic. Many of them, such as tar sands, make more pollution. And one day, these too will run out.**

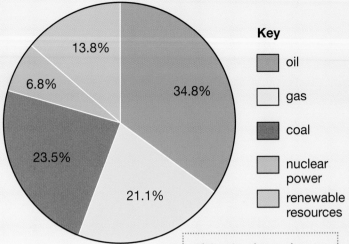

Key
- ☐ oil
- ☐ gas
- ☐ coal
- ☐ nuclear power
- ☐ renewable resources

13.8%
6.8%
34.8%
23.5%
21.1%

This pie chart shows where the world gets its energy at the moment. ⋀

FAST FACTS
- The world is using crude oil and natural gas as quickly as they can be taken from the ground.
- Scientists think that the world has already used half its supply of oil.

Not just fossil fuels

Different countries in different parts of the world get their energy in different ways. However, most countries use fossil fuels to supply almost all the energy they need. About 80 percent of the energy used in the world comes from fossil fuels.

billion one thousand million
nonrenewable will run out one day and cannot be replaced

What Next?

This car is fueled with liquid hydrogen. ∧

Fossil fuels are not just used as **energy resources.** They are important **raw materials.** Once the fossil fuels have gone, detergents, plastics, paints, and many other useful substances will have to be made from something else. Wood and natural oils found in plants will probably be used as raw materials. Plants are already being used as **fuels.**

Plant power

The seeds of some plants contain a lot of vegetable oil, which can be changed into "biodiesel." Just like diesel from **crude oil,** it can power buses and other vehicles. Sugar from sugarcane plants can be changed into ethanol. This liquid burns very easily. Ethanol on its own, or mixed with gasoline, is already being used as a fuel in some parts of Canada, Brazil, and the United States.

Go with hydrogen

Hydrogen is an explosive gas that burns very easily. It can be made from water or alcohols such as methanol. Hydrogen is difficult to store and handle, but water is the only waste from cars fueled by it. Scientists are working hard to make hydrogen easier to use.

Nuclear power stations make electricity without using fossil fuels. ∨

Word store　　atom　smallest particle of an element
geothermal　anything to do with heat from deep underground

Electric atoms

Everything is made from tiny bits called **atoms**. Some atoms are unstable, which means that they can break up into even smaller pieces. When they do this, they give out tiny amounts of **energy**. A lot of unstable atoms together can give out a lot of energy, including heat energy. This can be used to boil water to make steam, which can turn **turbines** and electricity **generators**.

Uranium is a metal with unstable atoms. It is used as a fuel in **nuclear** power stations. Unlike fossil fuels, uranium is not burned. But it does make harmful **radioactive** wastes. These give out invisible energy that can harm or even kill living things. Radioactive waste has to be handled and stored very carefully.

FAST FACTS
Supplies of uranium will run out in less than 50 years.

Hot rocks

Deep inside Earth, radioactive metals such as uranium give off heat energy. This makes the rocks very hot. **Geothermal** power stations use water heated naturally by these rocks to make electricity without making any harmful waste. Unfortunately, **suitable** hot rocks are not found everywhere in the world.

A geothermal power station in Iceland.

nuclear   using energy from atoms
radioactive   has atoms that give out harmful invisible energy

This is a solar generator in Australia. ⋁

Renewable energy resources

There are two main problems with **fossil fuels.** They are running out, and as they are used up, they **pollute** the atmosphere. **Renewable energy resources**, such as **solar** power and wind power, are different. They will not run out and they do not pollute the atmosphere.

Keep replanting

Wood is made from trees. Unlike the fossil fuels, which took millions of years to form, trees grow quickly. If forests are replanted as trees are cut down, there will always be supplies of wood. When wood burns, it gives off water **vapor** and carbon dioxide, just like fossil fuels. But carbon dioxide from burning wood does not increase the **greenhouse effect.** This is because trees also take carbon dioxide out of the atmosphere as they grow. The two effects balance each other out. Wood is already used to fuel some power stations.

Electricity from the Sun's heat

Solar power stations make electricity using the Sun's heat energy. Mirrors concentrate the heat onto one spot. In some designs this heat is turned directly into electricity. In other designs it boils water. The steam from the boiling water turns a turbine, which then turns an electricity generator.

FAST FACTS

Fuels made from living things are called biomass fuels.

Word store

blade   spinning arm on a windmill or turbine
hydroelectric power electricity made using the energy from moving water

Electricity from movement

It is possible to power electricity **generators** without burning any **fuel.** The wind, waves, and tides are already moving, and their kinetic **energy** can turn electricity generators. Wind **turbines** have long **blades** that spin in the wind. The spinning blades turn generators to make electricity. Water flowing in a river, or falling from behind a **dam,** can be sent through pipes to turbines. The moving water turns the turbines, which then turn generators.

A tidal power station uses the moving seawater to turn turbines and generators. These are arranged in a long dam built across a bay or river mouth. Wave-power machines **use the up-and-down movement in waves to make electricity.**

Solar cells on houses in the Netherlands. ∧

Electricity from the Sun's light

Solar cells change light into electricity. A few small solar cells can power a calculator, but lots of them working together can do much more. Solar cells make electricity for traffic signs and telephone booths in **remote** places. Some even make enough electricity for a whole house.

Electricity can be generated using water rushing down from high up behind a dam. Electricity made from moving water is called **hydroelectric power.** ∧

Keep looking

It will be many years before all our electricity can be made without **fossil fuels.** The alternative **energy resources** have problems of their own.

- **Nuclear** power stations take much longer to get started. They can provide a certain amount of electricity all the time, but they cannot make extra electricity quickly enough to meet a sudden rise in demand. The supply of uranium fuel for nuclear power stations will also run out one day.
- Although **hydroelectric power** stations can start making electricity quickly, at any time, wind **turbines** only make electricity on windy days.
- **Solar** power stations do not work at night when it is dark.

New oilfields are usually in **remote** places, buried deep underground. ⋀

As fossil fuels run out, they get harder to take out of Earth. New roads, pipelines, refineries, and ports damage the environment in wild and beautiful places, and oil may be spilled by accident.

When oil tankers have accidents at sea, birds and other animals get covered in thick, sticky oil. ➤

Word store   fuel cell   device that makes electricity from fuels such as hydrogen and methanol

In the future, all the different ways to generate electricity will have to be used together to produce the electricity we need. Until then, scientists and engineers will keep looking for new supplies of fossil fuels and ways to use **renewable** energy resources.

Fossil fuels

Benefits

- Even small amounts of fossil fuels have a lot of stored chemical energy in them. This is easily released as heat and light energy by burning.
- Power stations running on fossil fuels are easily and quickly started.
- **Coal** is easily **transported** by trucks, trains, or ships.
- **Natural gas** can be moved along pipelines and stored as either a gas or a liquid.

Problems

- The liquid fuels from **crude oil** are dangerous to transport because they can catch fire easily.
- Fossil fuels are **nonrenewable**, so they will run out one day.
- They cause **pollution** when they burn, which harms living things and adds to **global warming**. Taking fossil fuels out of the ground, and accidents with oil tankers, damages the environment.

No cars in the future?

When crude oil runs out, there will be no gasoline or diesel to fuel cars. Scientists are studying different ways to power cars. Some new designs run on methanol, ethanol, or hydrogen. Some use more than one fuel. These could be the cars of the future.

A **fuel cell** in this electric car makes electricity using hydrogen fuel. ◁

Find Out More

Organizations

Understanding Energy

Information and quizzes about **energy** and generating electricity

energy.org.uk

Fossil fuels

Lots of information about the fossil fuels

fe.doe.gov/education/

Pollution and fuels

Great site on **pollution** topics including air quality, **acid rain,** and **global warming**

doc.mmu.ac.uk/aric/eae/

Books

Oxlade, Chris. *Science Topics: Energy*. Chicago: Heinemann Library, 2000.

Parker, Steve. *Energy Files: Water, Solar, Wind*. Chicago: Heinemann Library, 2002.

Saunders, Nigel, and Steven Chapman. *Energy Essentials: Renewable Energy*. Chicago: Raintree, 2004.

Sneddon, Robert. *Energy for Life: Fossil Fuels*. Chicago: Heinemann Library, 2002.

World Wide Web

If you want to find out more about **fossil fuels,** you can search the Internet using keywords such as these:

- "fossil fuels"
- coal + mining
- oil + refining
- oil + uses
- "tar pit"
- "natural gas"

You can also make your own keywords by using headings or words from this book. Use the search tips opposite to help you find the most useful websites.

Search tips

There are billions of pages on the Internet, so it can be difficult to find exactly what you want to find. For example, if you just type in "energy" on a search engine such as Google, you will get a list of 35 million web pages. These search skills will help you find useful websites more quickly:

- Use simple keywords instead of whole sentences.
- Use two to six keywords in a search, putting the most important words first.
- Be precise—only use names of people, places, or things.
- If you want to find words that go together, put quotation marks around them—for example "tidal power" or "wind energy."
- Use the advanced section of your search engine.
- Use the "+" sign between keywords to link them.

Where to search

Search engine

A search engine looks through the entire web and lists all sites that match the words in the search box. It can give thousands of links, but the best matches are at the top of the list, on the first page. Try **www.google.com**.

Search directory

A search directory is like a library of websites that have been sorted by a person instead of a computer. You can search by keyword or subject and browse through the different sites like you look through books on a library shelf. A good example is **yahooligans.com**.

Glossary

acidic   has a pH below 7

acid rain   rain that contains more acid than normal; it damages buildings and living things

Arctic   far north, where it is usually very cold

atom   smallest particle in an element

bacteria   tiny living things

barrel   unit used to measure the volume of crude oil; one barrel is 42 gallons (159 liters)

billion   one thousand million

blade   spinning arm on a windmill or turbine

blowout   dangerous and uncontrolled escape of oil from a well

bog   waterlogged and spongy wetland

carboniferous   coal-producing

Carboniferous period   period of time from 360 to 280 million years ago

catalytic converter   equipment added to a vehicle exhaust system to reduce the amount of harmful gases given out

chemical reaction   change in which new substances are made

chlorophyll   green substance that absorbs light energy; it is found in plants

coal   black solid fossil fuel

coalface   part of a coal seam that is being cut away

compressor   type of pump

condense   to change from gas to liquid

crude oil   liquid fossil fuel with various solids and gases dissolved in it

crust   rocky outer layer of Earth

dam   barrier built across a river to block it so that water can be stored

density   measure of how heavy something is compared to its size

dilute   mixed with another substance, usually water

dissolve   to mix completely with water to make a solution

efficient   good at doing useful things with the energy it gets

element   substance made of only one kind of atom

energy   ability to do work; light, heat, and electricity are types of energy

energy resource   something from which we can get useful amounts of energy

evaporate   to change from liquid into gas

extract   remove or take out

fertilizer   chemical that gives plants the minerals they need to grow well

fossil fuel   fuel formed from the remains of ancient plants and animals

fossilized   turned into stone

fraction   group of substances in crude oil

fuel cell   device that makes electricity from fuels such as hydrogen and methanol

fuel   substance that stores energy and releases it when it is burned

generator   equipment used to make electricity

geologist   scientist who studies rocks

geothermal   anything to do with heat from deep underground

global warming   extra warming of Earth caused by an increased greenhouse effect

glucose   type of sugar, an important energy store for living things

greenhouse effect how Earth's atmosphere keeps the planet warm

hydrocarbon substance made from hydrogen and carbon only

hydroelectric power electricity made using the energy from moving water

ice age time when a lot of Earth was covered by ice

landfill waste site

lubricate to reduce friction

mine dig out of the ground

mineral substance needed by plants and animals to keep them healthy

molecule tiny piece of matter made from atoms stuck together

natural gas colorless fossil fuel gas, mostly methane

neutralize make a substance neutral so it does not react with metals or rocks

nonporous does not let liquids and gases through

nonrenewable will run out one day and can never be replaced

nuclear using energy from atoms

patent protect by law so that other people cannot steal the inventor's ideas

pest insect or fungus that damages plants

pesticide chemical that kills insects and other pests that harm crops

photosynthesis process by which plants use light energy to convert carbon dioxide and water into sugars and oxygen

poisonous substance that makes us ill or even kills us

polar ice caps ice covering the north and south poles of Earth

pollute to add harmful substances to the air, water, or land

pollution harmful substances in the air, water, or on land

porous lets liquids and gases through

radioactive has atoms that give out harmful invisible energy

rank type of coal

raw material substance that is turned into a final product

reclaim to make something useful again

remote far away from towns and cities

renewable will not run out and can be replaced

seam layer of coal

shaft narrow vertical hole

smog mixture of smoke and fog

solar anything to do with the Sun

spoil heap pile of waste material from a mine

subside sink downward

suitable right for the job

technician someone who helps scientists do their work

transport take or carry

trillion one thousand billion

turbine machinery that is turned by moving air, water, or steam

ultraviolet light invisible light that can damage skin, eyes, and growing plants

valve device for controlling the movement of liquid or gas through a pipe

vapor gas

wire gauze fine metal mesh

Index